Swing With A Band

Music Minus One

8064

SUGGESTIONS FOR USING THIS MMO EDITION

WE HAVE TRIED to create a product that will provide you an easy way to learn and perform these compositions with a full ensemble in the comfort of your own home. The following MMO features and techniques will help you maximize the effectiveness of the MMO practice and performance system:

Because it involves a fixed accompaniment performance, there is an inherent lack of flexibility in tempo. We have observed generally accepted tempi, and always in the originally intended key, but some may wish to perform at a different tempo, or to slow down or speed up the accompaniment for practice purposes; or to alter the piece to a more comfortable key. You can purchase from MMO specialized CD players & recorders which allow variable speed while maintaining proper pitch, and vice versa. This is an indispensable tool for the serious musician and you may wish to look into purchasing this useful piece of equipment for full enjoyment of all your MMO editions.

We want to provide you with the most useful practice and performance accompaniments possible. If you have any suggestions for improving the MMO system, please feel free to contact us. You can reach us by e-mail at *info@musicminusone.com*.

MUSIC MINUS ONE

8064

Contents

DON'T BE THAT WAY

Benny Goodman, Mitchell Parish
and Edgar Sampson

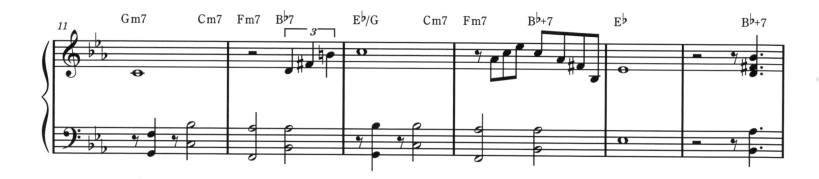

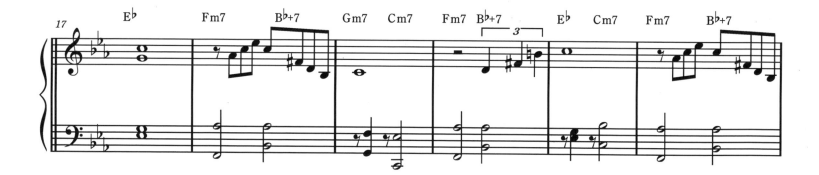

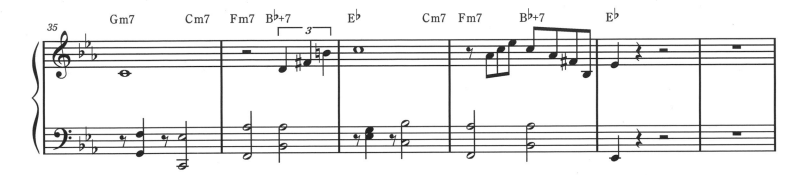

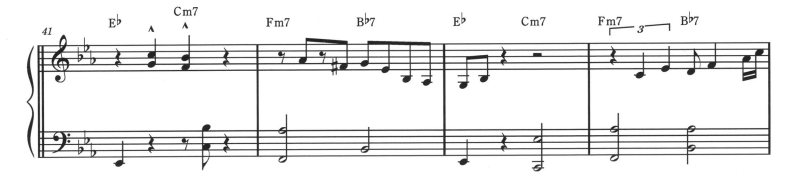

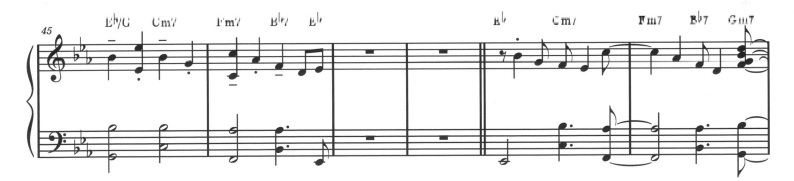

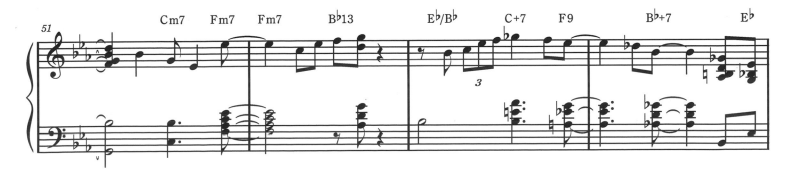

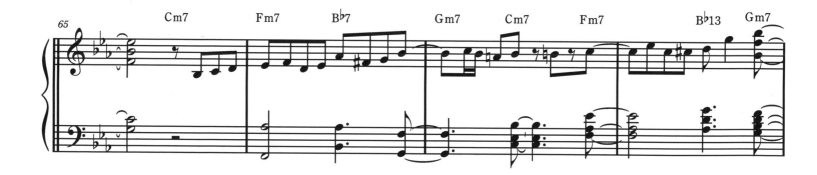

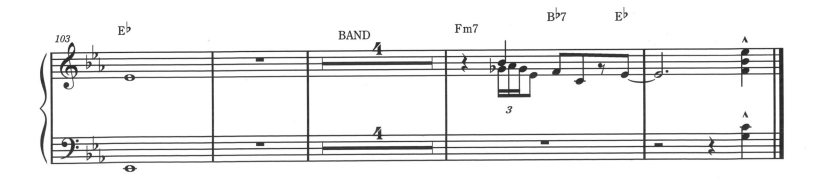

I'M THROUGH WITH LOVE

Matt Malneck, Bud Livingston
and Gus Kahn

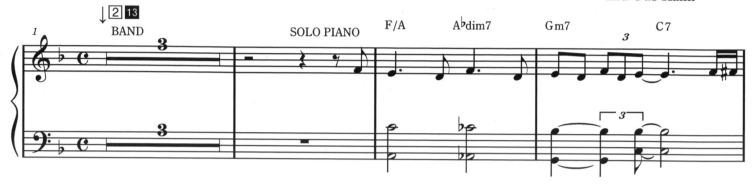

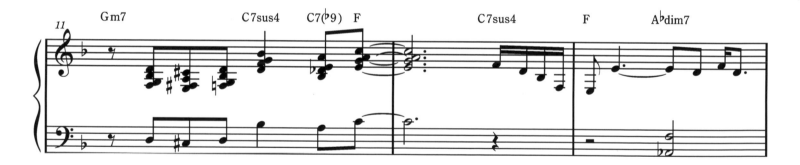

I'M THROUGH WITH LOVE
Words by GUS KAHN Music by MATT MALNECK and BUD LIVINGSTON
© 1931 (Renewed) METRO-GOLDWYN-MAYER INC.
Rights for the Extended Renewal Term in the U.S.
Controlled by GILBERT KEYES MUSIC COMPANY and EMI ROBBINS CATALOG INC.
All Rights for GILBERT KEYES MUSIC COMPANY Administered by WB MUSIC CORP.
All Rights Reserved   Used by Permission of ALFRED PUBLISHING CO., INC.

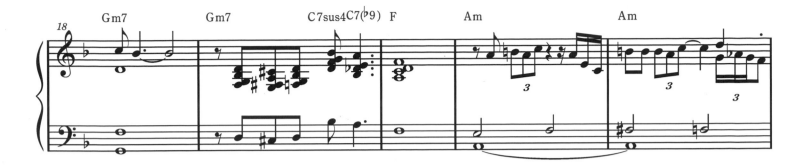

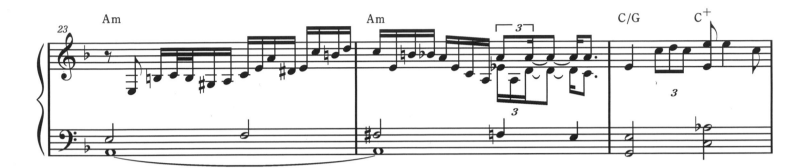

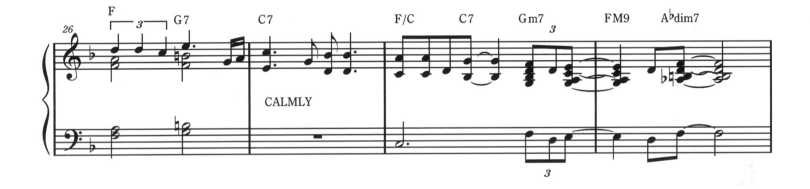

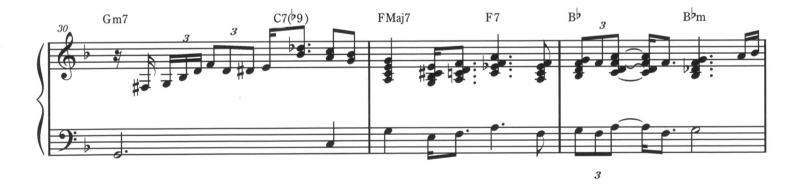

ROSE ROOM

Harry Williams and Art Hickman

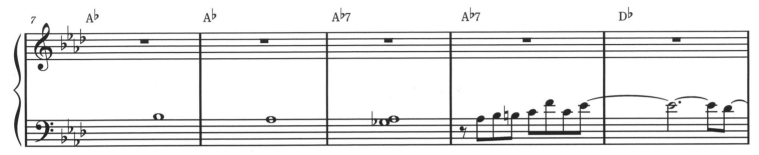

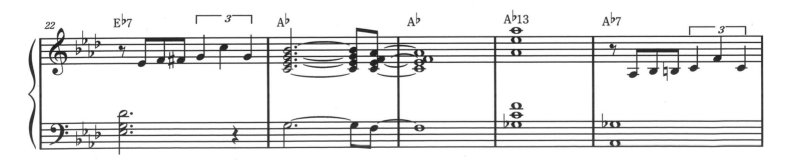

ROSE ROOM
Harry Williams and Art Hickman

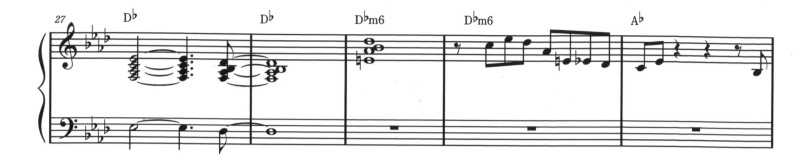

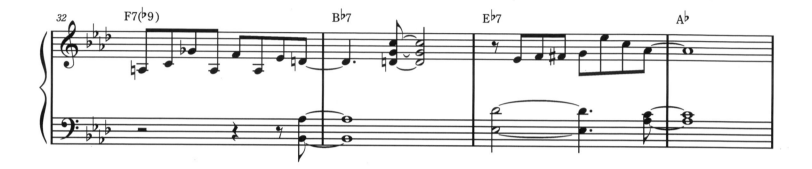

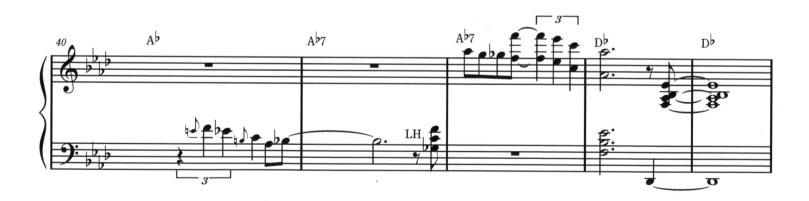

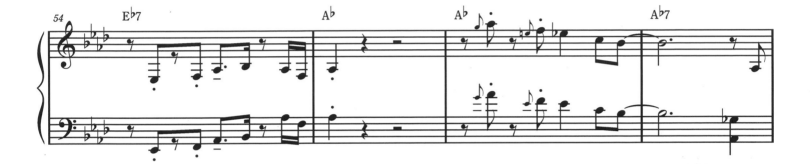

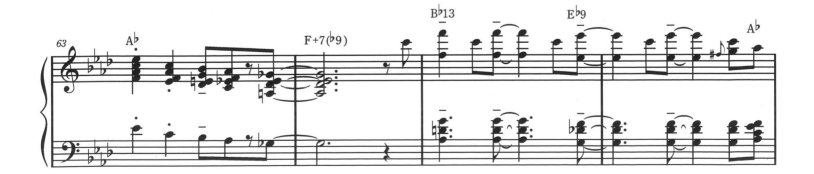

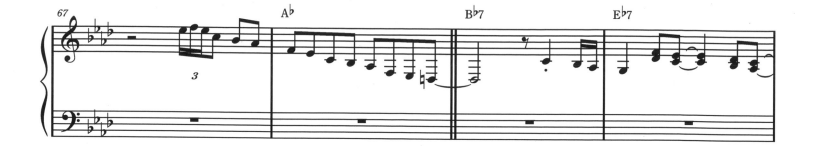

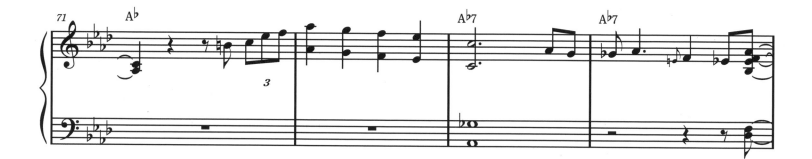

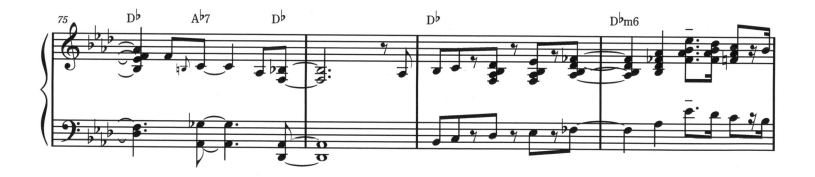

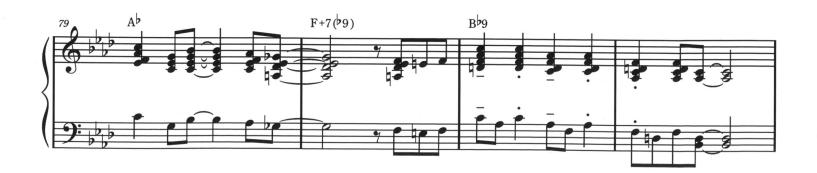

MMO 8064

I'LL NEVER BE THE SAME

Gus Kahn, Matt Malneck
and Frank Signorelli

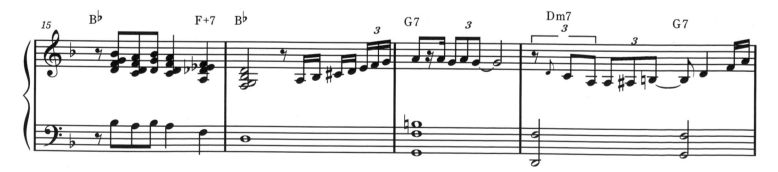

I'LL NEVER BE THE SAME
By GUS KAHN, MATT MALNECK and FRANK SIGNORELLI
© 1932 (Renewed 1960) EMI ROBBINS CATALOG INC.
All Rights Controlled by EMI ROBBINS CATALOG INC. (Publishing)
and ALFRED PUBLISHING CO., INC. (Print)
All Rights Reserved   Used by Permission

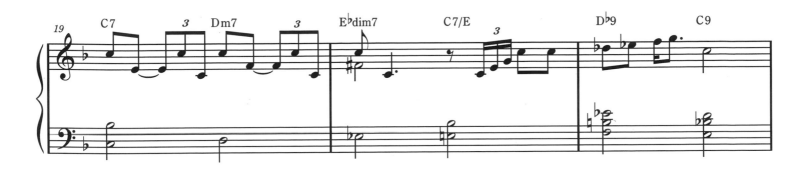

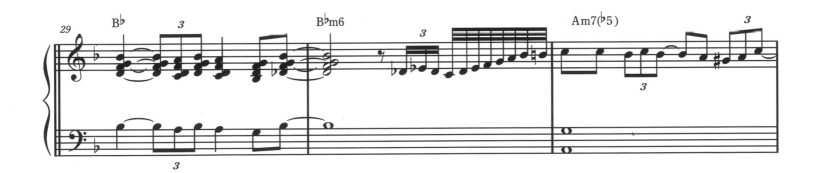

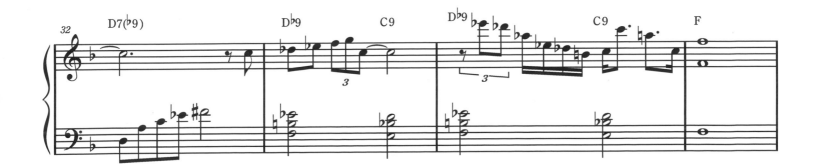

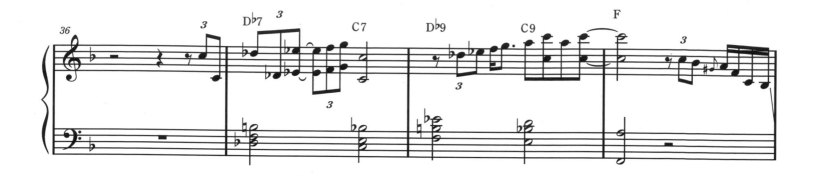

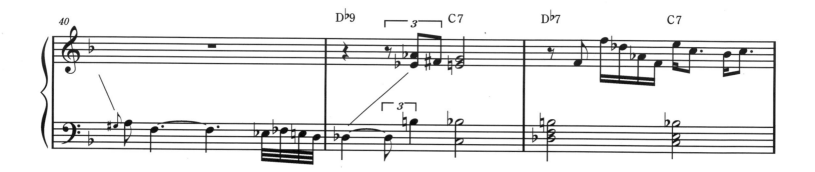

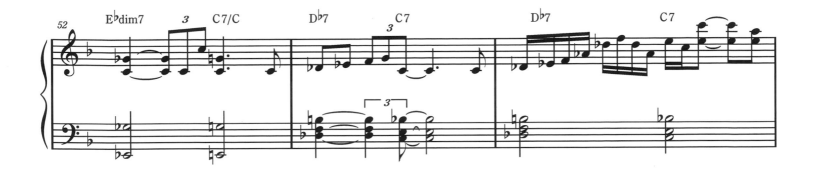

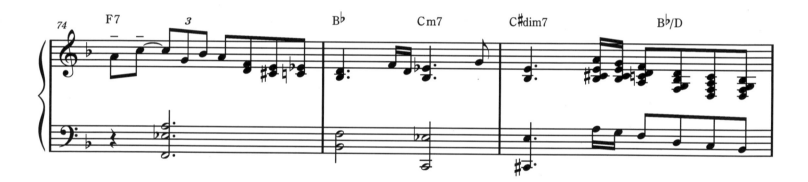

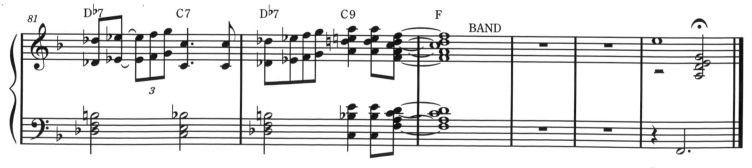

HOW AM I TO KNOW?

Dorothy Parker and Jack King

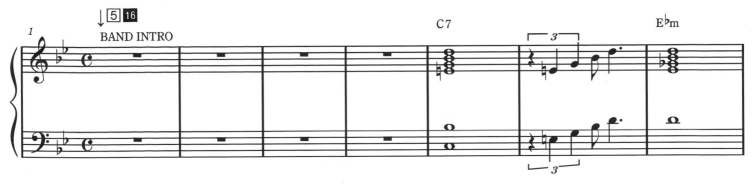

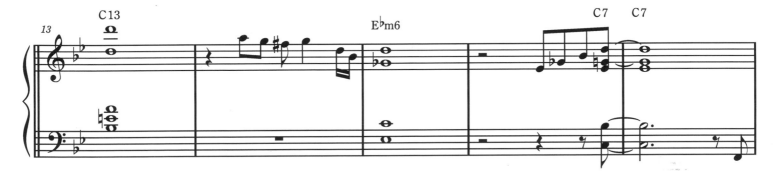

HOW AM I TO KNOW? (from "Dynamite")
Words by DOROTHY PARKER Music by JACK KING
© 1929 (Renewed) EMI ROBBINS CATALOG, INC.
All Rights Controlled by EMI ROBBINS CATALOG, INC. (Publishing)
and ALFRED PUBLISHING CO., INC. (Print)
All Rights Reserved   Used by Permission

MMO 8064

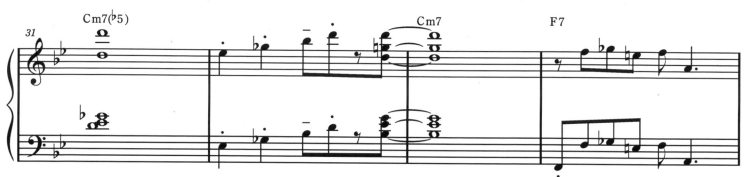

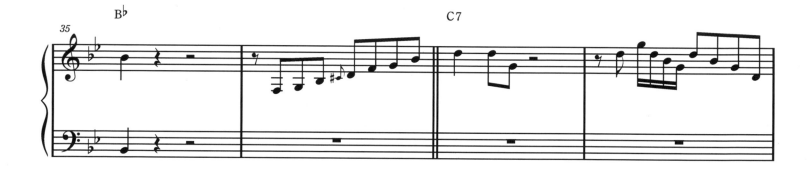

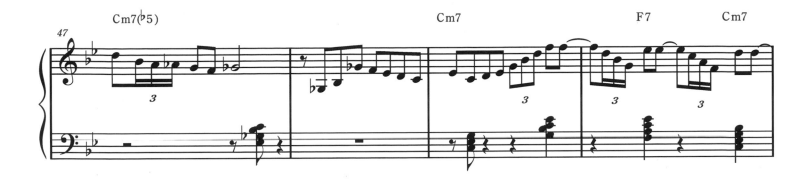

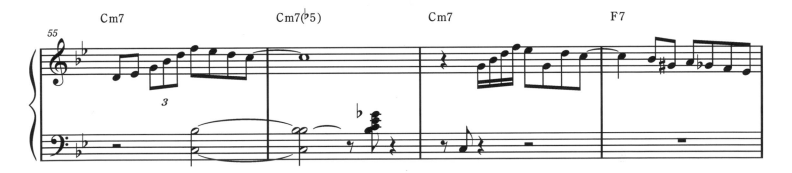

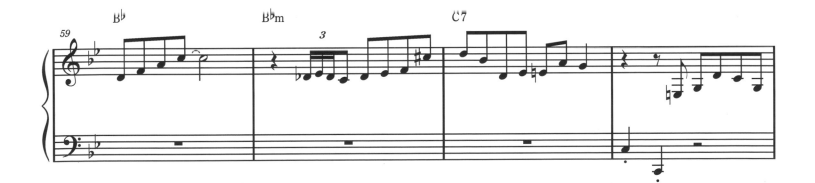

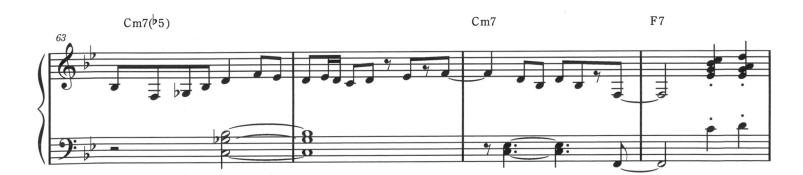

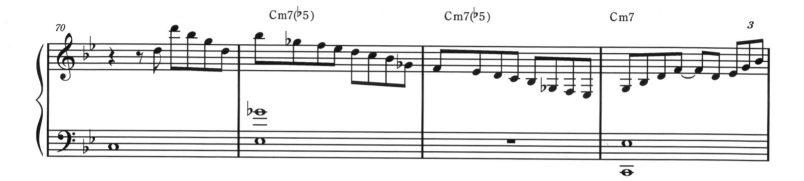

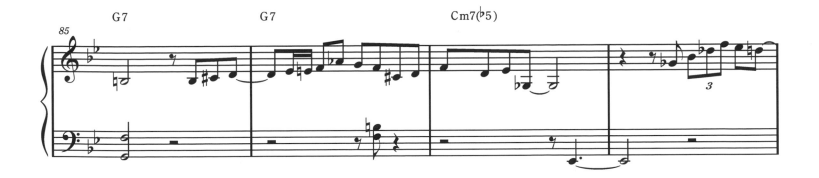

STOMPIN' AT THE SAVOY

Benny Goodman, Edgar Sampson, Chick Webb
and Andy Razaf

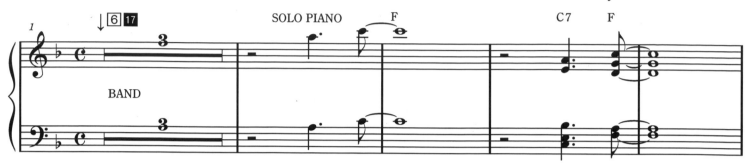

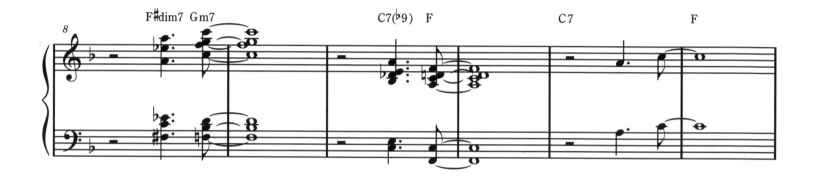

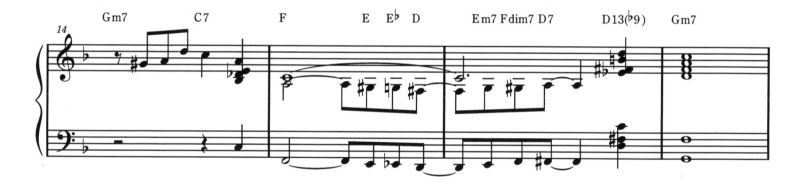

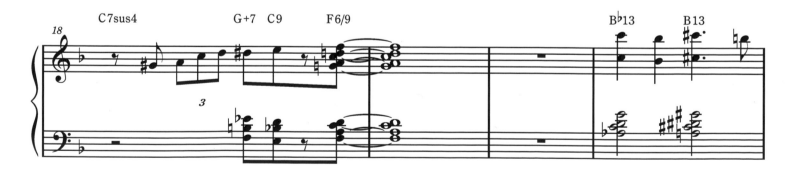

STOMPIN' AT THE SAVOY
Words by Andy Razaf
Music by Benny Goodman, Edgar Sampson and Chick Webb
Copyright ©1936 by EMI Robbins Catalog Inc.
Copyright Renewed by Rytvoc, Inc., Ragbag Music Publishing Corporation (ASCAP), EMI Robbins Music Corporation and Razaf Music Co.
This arrangement Copyright ©2008 by Rytvoc, Inc., Ragbag Music Publishing Corporation (ASCAP),
EMI Robbins Music Corporation and Razaf Music Co.
International Copyright Secured   All Rights Reserved   Used by Permission

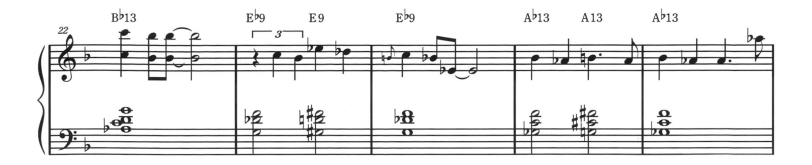

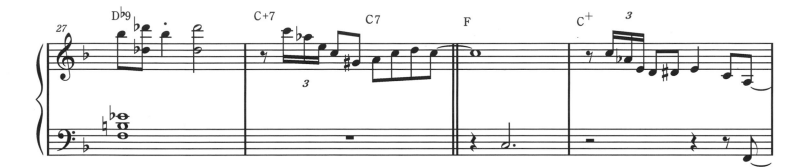

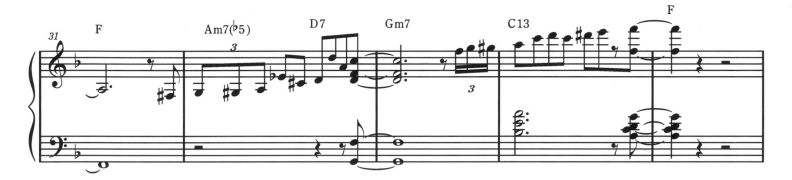

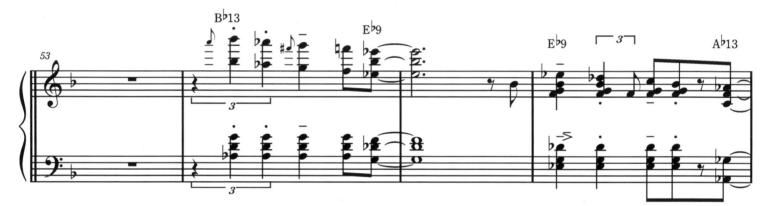

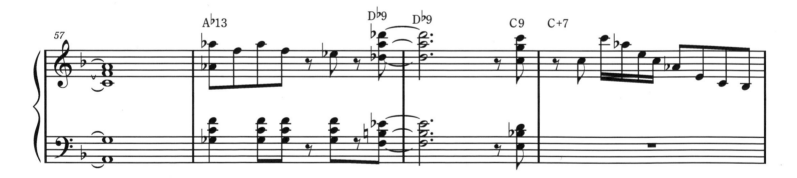

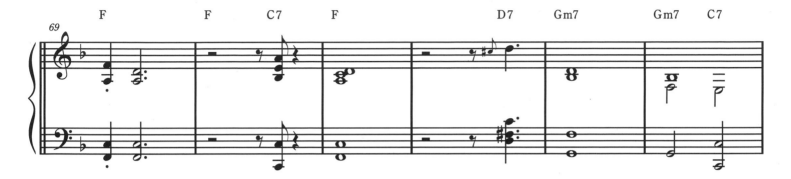

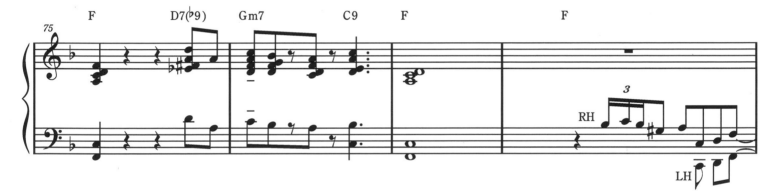

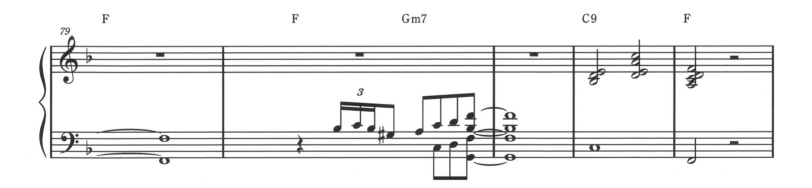

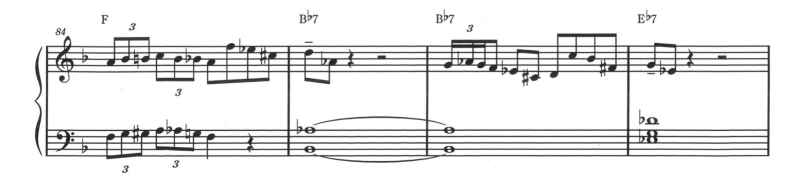

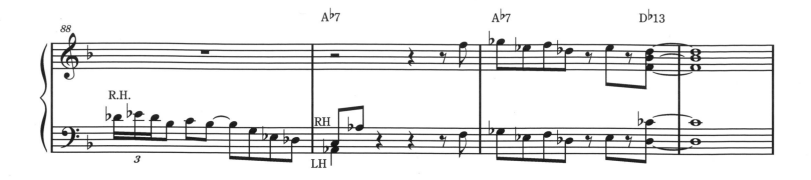

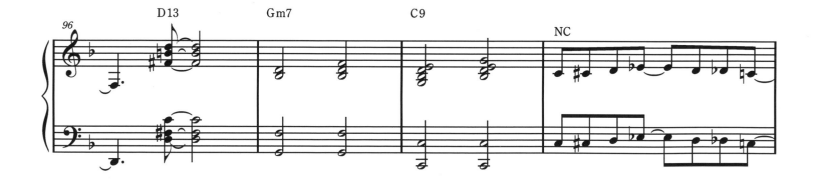

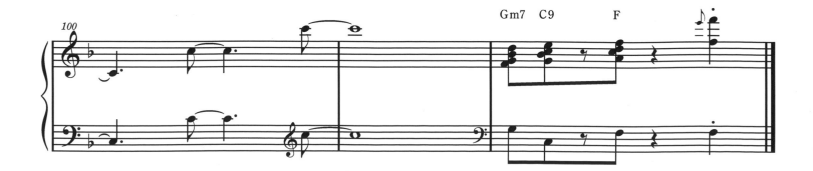

I UNDERSTAND

Kim Gannon and Mabel Wayne

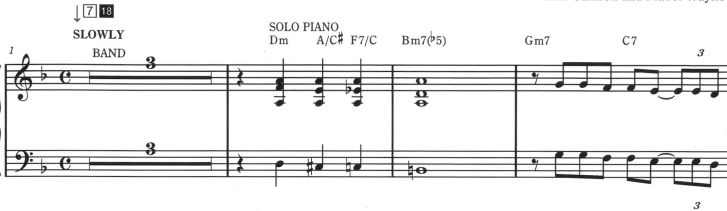

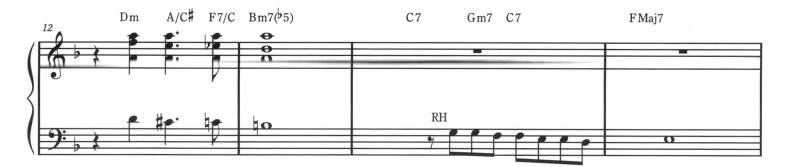

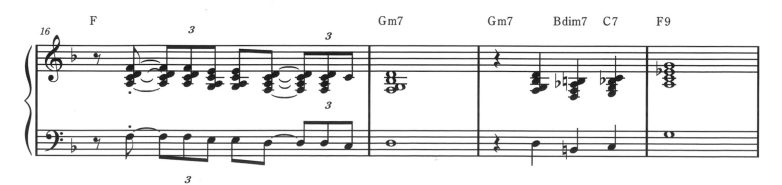

I UNDERSTAND
Lyrics by KIM GANNON Music by MABEL WAYNE

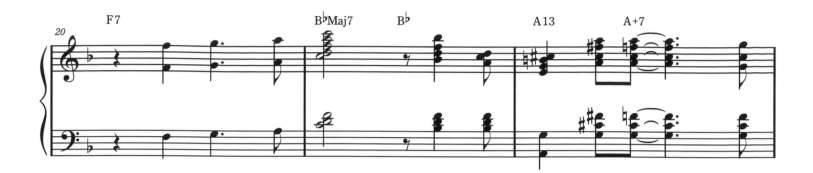

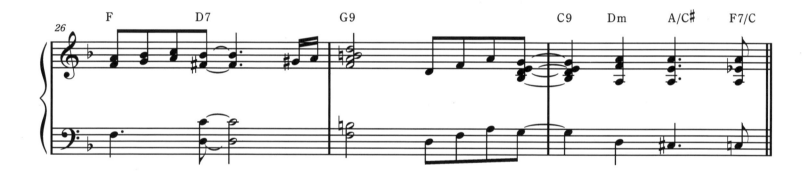

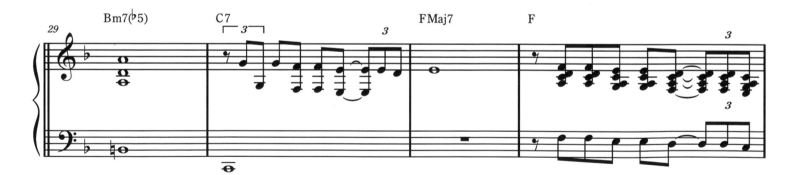

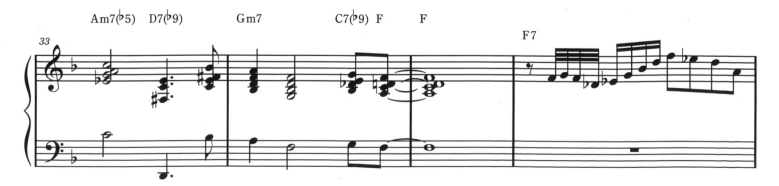

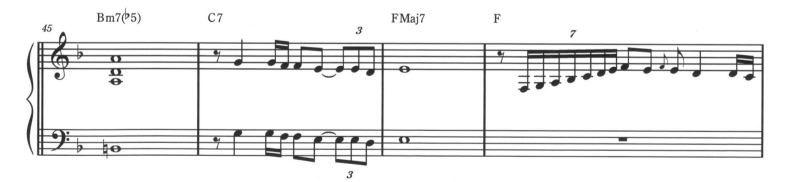

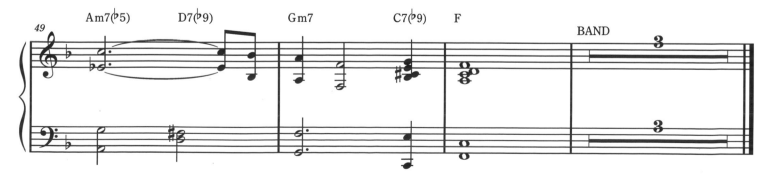

WHAT CAN I SAY AFTER I SAY I'M SORRY

Walter Donaldson and Abe Lyman

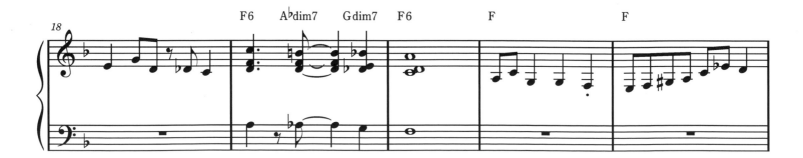

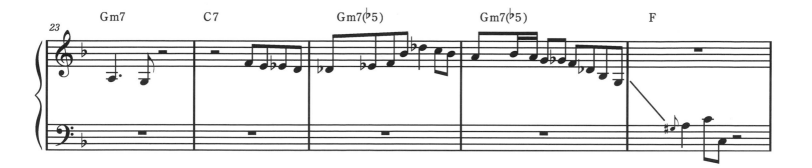

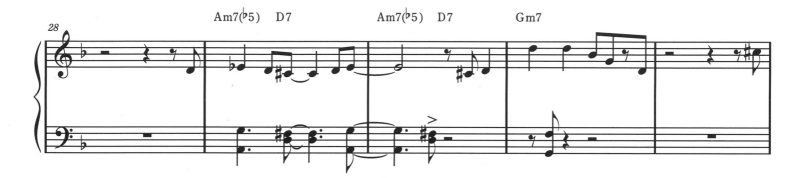

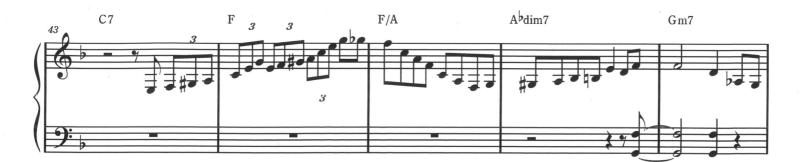

MMO 8064

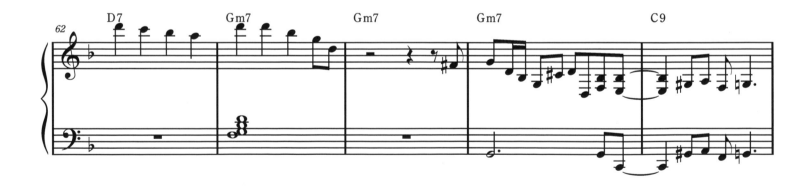

Option: Play top notes only to end of phrase

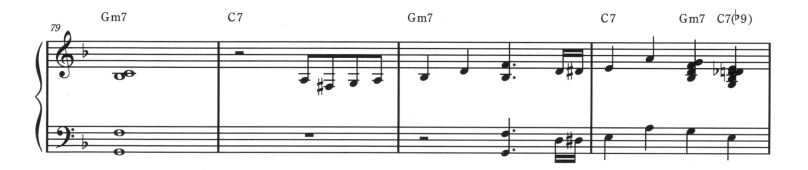

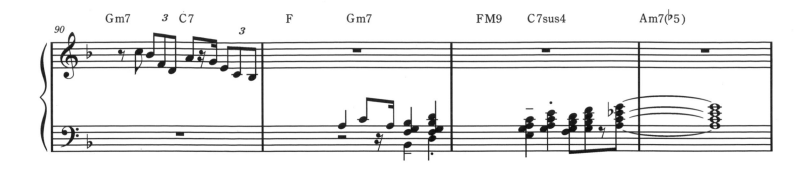

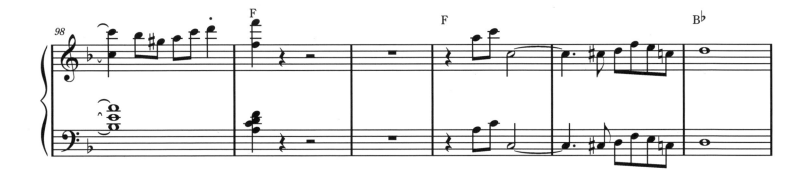

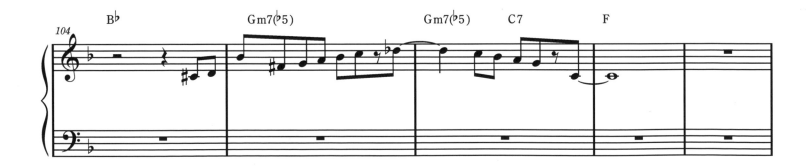

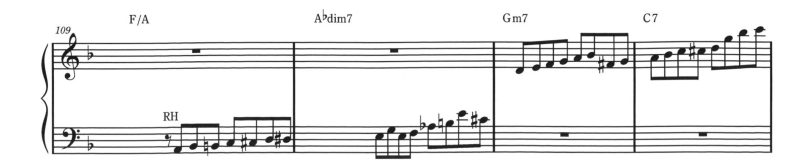

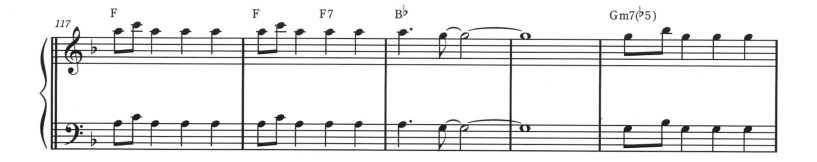

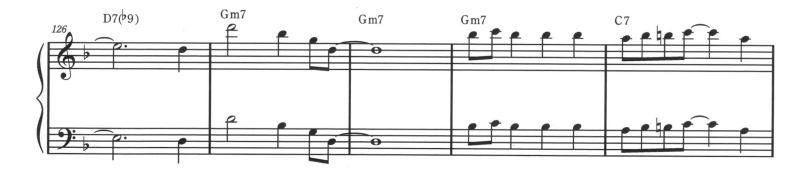

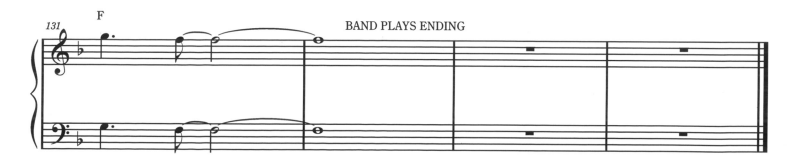

BAND PLAYS ENDING

I'M IN THE MOOD FOR LOVE

Jimmy McHugh and Dorothy Fields

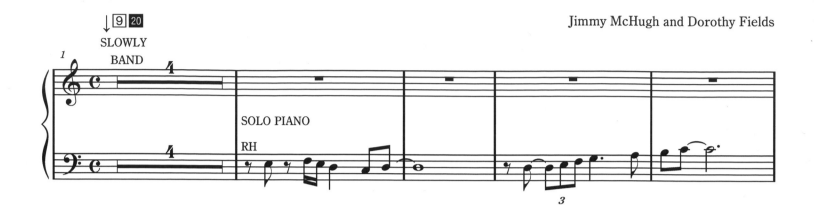

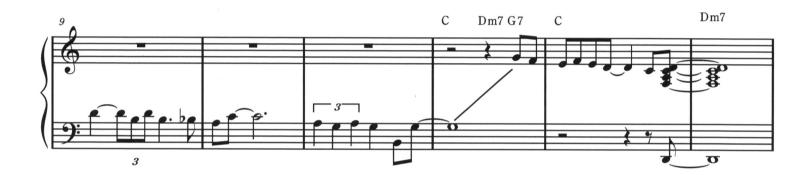

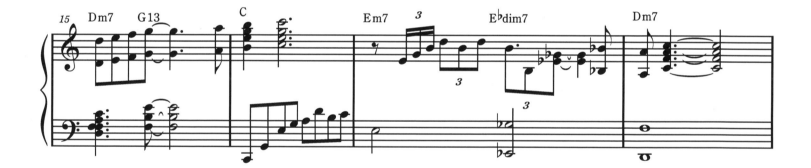

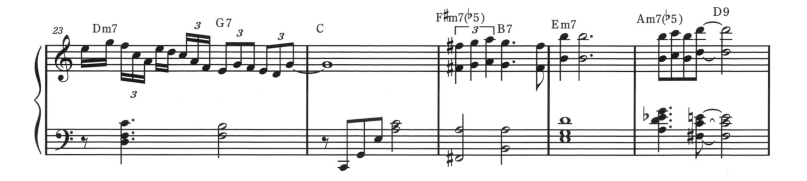

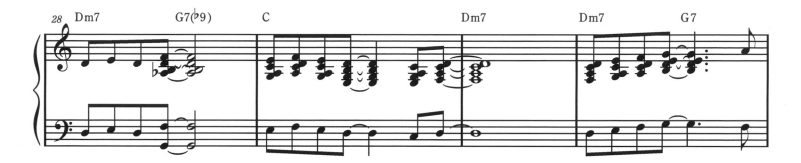

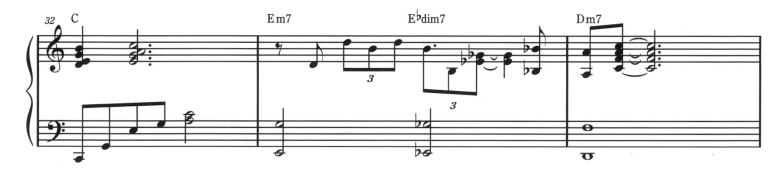

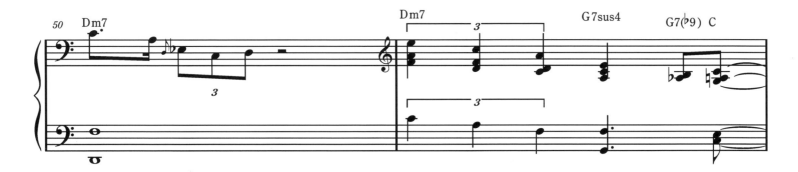

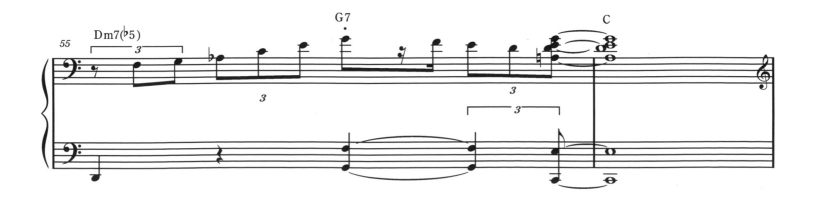

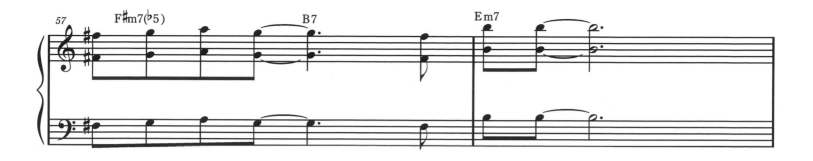

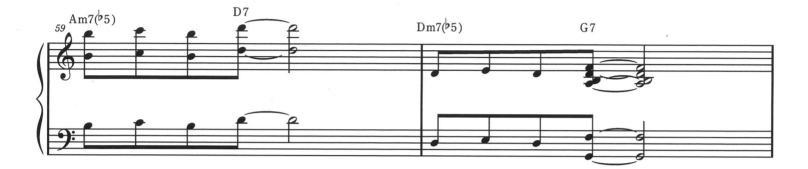

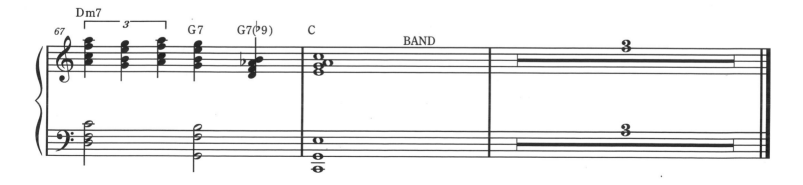

I GOT IT BAD
(And That Ain't Good)

Duke Ellington and Paul Francis Webster

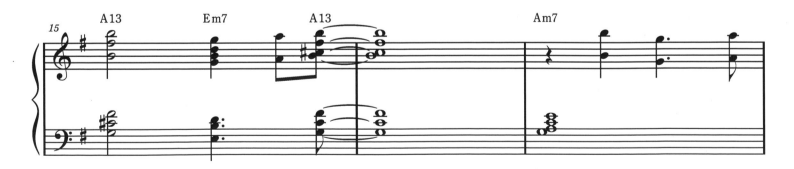

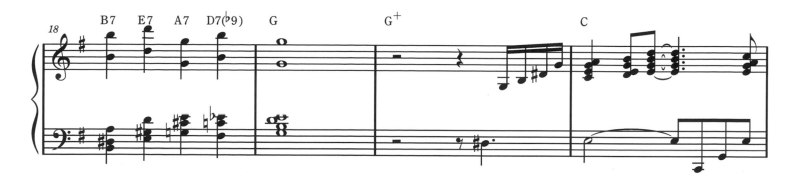

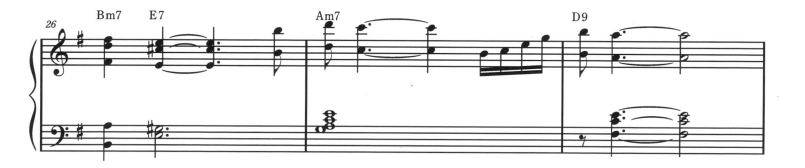

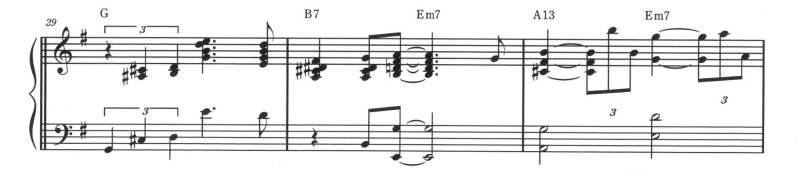

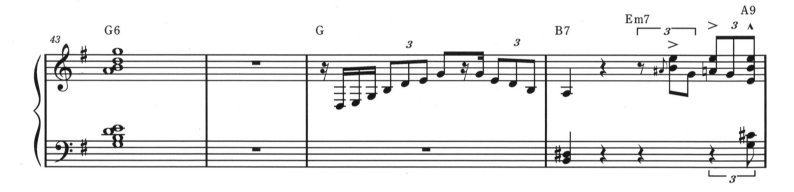

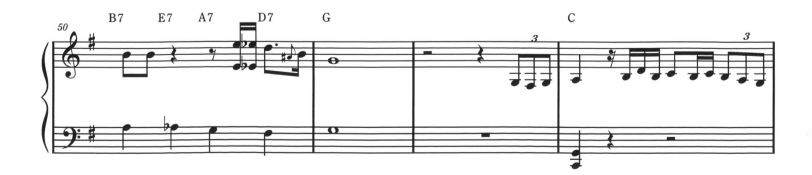

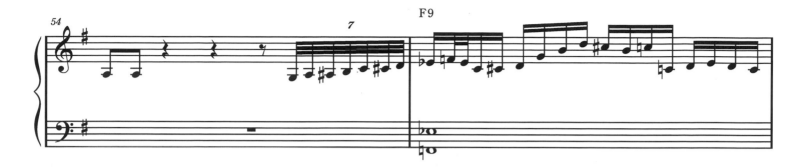

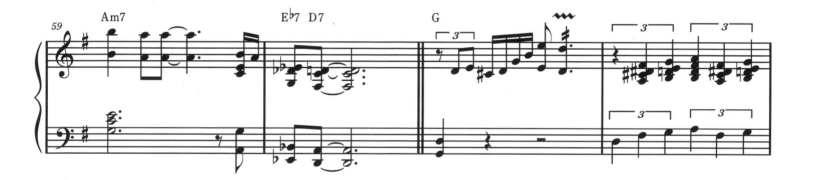

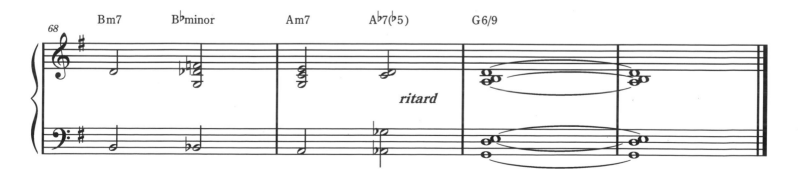

MMO 8064

ONE O'CLOCK JUMP

Count Basie

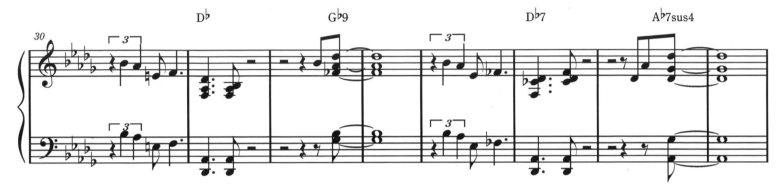

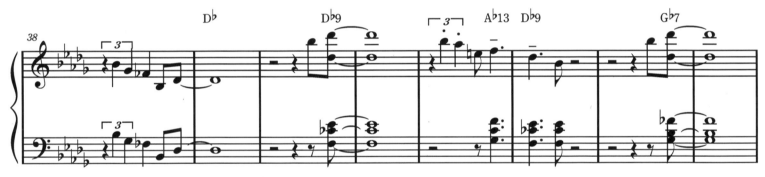

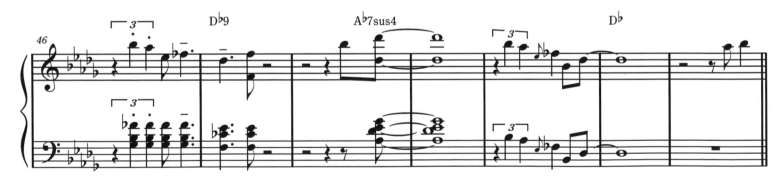

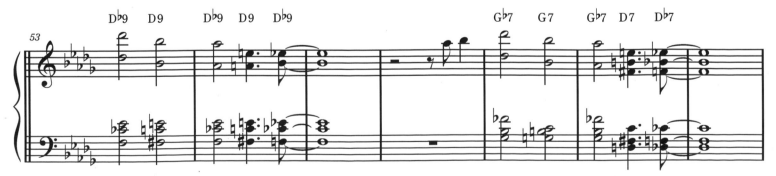

ONE O'CLOCK JUMP
Music by COUNT BASIE
© 1938 (Renewed) EMI FEIST CATALOG INC.
All Rights Controlled by EMI FEIST CATALOG INC. (Publishing)
and ALFRED PUBLISHING CO., INC. (Print)
All Rights Reserved

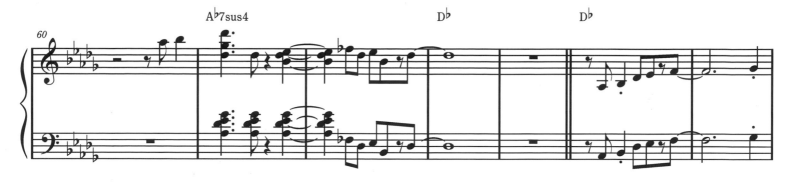

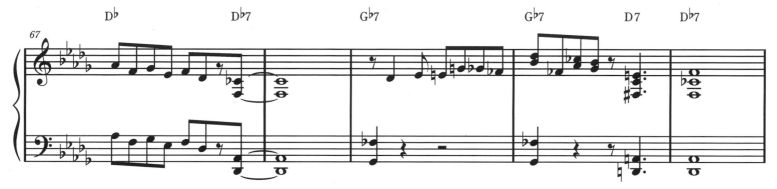

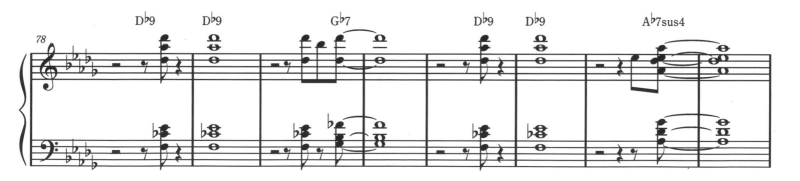

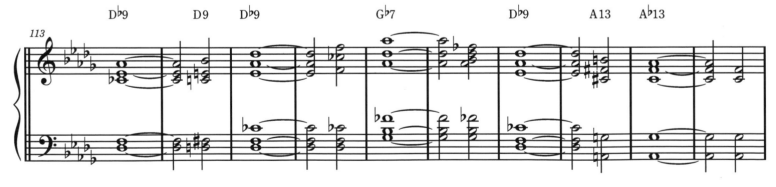

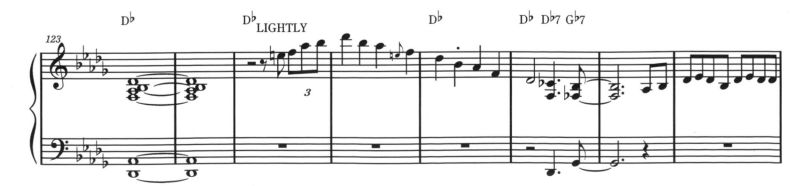

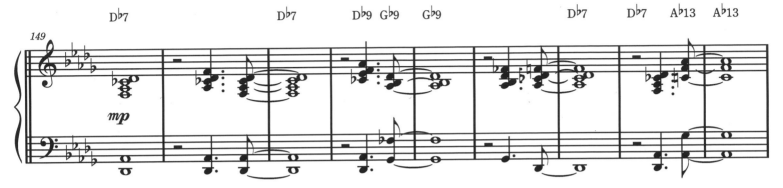

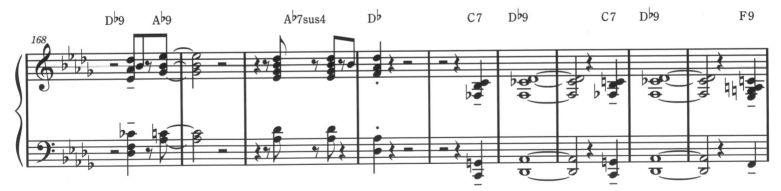

MUSIC MINUS ONE
50 Executive Boulevard
Elmsford, New York 10523-1325
800-669-7464 (U.S.)/914-592-1188 (International)

www.musicminusone.com
e-mail: info@musicminusone.com